THIS MANUAL IS THE EXCLUSIVE
PROPERTY OF THE SUPREME PONTIFF OF
THE ROMAN CATHOLIC CHURCH

....

signas hic (sign here)

THE POPE

HOW TO BE

Pope

HOW TO BE

WHAT TO DO AND WHERE TO GO
ONCE YOU'RE IN THE VATICAN

Piers Marchant

CHRONICLE BOOKS
SAN FRANCISCO

Library of Congress Cataloging-in-Publication Data available.

ISBN: 0-8118-5221-0

Manufactured in the United States of America

Designed by Lynne Yeamans and Nancy Leonard
Illustrations by Rodica Prato © 2005
Cover illustration © Peter Harholdt/CORBIS
Typeset in Agincourt, Centaur, and Helvetica Neue

A QUIRK Packaging Book
www.quirkpackaging.com

Distributed in the U.K. by Hi Marketing
38 Carver Road
London SE2 49LT

Distributed in Canada by Raincoast Books
9050 Shaughnessy Street
Vancouver, British Columbia V6P 6E5

10 9 8 7 6 5 4 3 2 1

Chronicle Books LLC
85 Second Street
San Francisco, California 94105
www.chroniclebooks.com

✠

And I say also unto thee, that thou art Peter,
and upon this rock I will build my church;
and the gates of hell shall not prevail against it.

—MATTHEW 16:15–19

Despite the great difficulties, I accept.

—JOHN PAUL II, PONTIFF

Contents

✤

INTRODUCTION

Congratulations, Your Holiness,

and welcome to your first day at the Holy See.

The long line of popes remains largely unbroken after nearly two millennia. Only the emperor of Japan can claim to have a longer succession. As head of the Holy See—which encompasses the government of Vatican City and the Roman Catholic church, including the College of Cardinals and all the various sections and departments of the Roman Curia—you are now the most powerful figure in the church, speaking for more than one billion members worldwide. It's an enormous responsibility, but the cardinals convened their conclave and decreed that you were just the person for the job.

And with this manual in hand, you will walk into

your position confident and well informed. While the church has long maintained an aura of complete secrecy to outsiders, this manual—compiled over the last 2,000 years—is the ultimate insider's guide. Assisted by dozens of helpful diagrams and illustrations, the manual's recurring sections give you the crucial information and guidance you'll need to fulfill your papal duties and obligations. You'll find the intricacies of the job broken down into small, useful nuggets of information (Essential Papal Knowledge); collections of historical anecdotes, facts, and figures that will help round out your understanding of particular papal subjects (For Your Holiness's Information); and frank answers to Frequently Asked Questions. Frequently used abbreviations are the VC for the Vatican City and JP II for Pope John Paul II.

Urbi et orbi.

Vatican City

Vatican Gardens

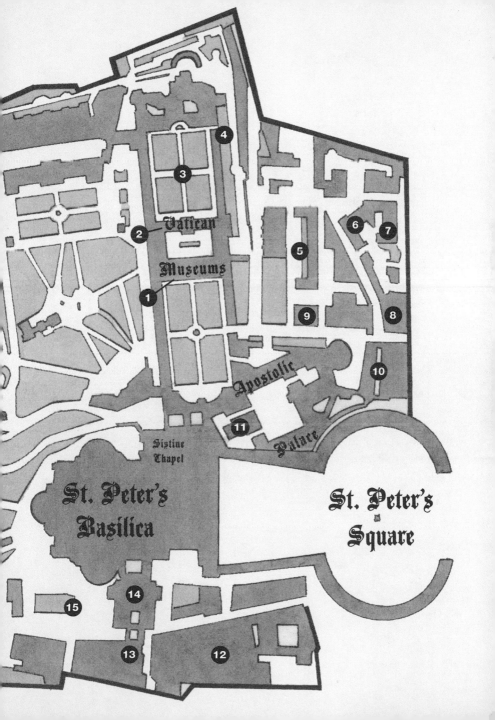

CHAPTER I

Getting Settled

You are the "rock" of the church and the successor to St. Peter—the single most visible symbol of the Catholic faith for more than one billion church followers around the globe. You are also the CEO of the church, maintaining order within an organization that has lasted through the millennia. And finally, you are in charge of the church's own city-state, Vatican City. It's a lot of responsibility, but it's important not to get too far ahead of yourself when you're starting out. To begin with, you've got to get yourself settled into your new position and living space.

Essential Papal Knowledge

CHOOSING YOUR NAME

Your papal name is different from your birth name and is intended to signify the new life you will lead as the head of the Holy See. This tradition began in 533 when John II, whose given name was Mercurius, decided that his name was too close to the name of the pagan god Mercury. Generally, new popes have chosen their papal name in homage to previous popes, saints, or apostles—excluding Peter, the first pope, whose name has never been used again. Since John Paul I, you also have the option of choosing two names and starting over numerically.

For Your Holiness's Information

SINGULAR OR PLURAL?

Throughout the history of the office, popes have generally employed the third person and the royal plural to refer to themselves as a way of conveying the significance of their office. John Paul I, the self-effacing "smiling pontiff," was, in fact, the first to cease using the royal "we" when speaking about himself. John Paul II (JP II) continued this practice, keeping to the far more humble first-person "I," while Benedict XVI has returned to the traditional form of papal self-reference, again employing the royal plural. If you're still not sure which you would like to select, stand in front of a mirror and practice saying "I would like a sandwich" and "We would like a sandwich" and see which suits you better.

PAPAL NAME STATS

Some of the most frequently and infrequently used papal names:

John (XXIII), the most popular
Gregory (XVI)
Benedict (XVI)
Linus (I)
Soter (I)
Theodore (I)

NATIONALITIES OF POPES

The 264 popes who have followed St. Peter (or 262 to be exact, since Benedict IX was elected three times during the church's turbulent medieval period) include . . .

---

205 Italians (106 Romans)
19 French
14 Greeks
8 Syrians
6 Germans
3 Africans
2 Spaniards
1 each: Austrian, Polish, Palestinian, English, and Dutch

Frequently Asked Questions

**WHO WAS POPE FOR THE LONGEST TIME?
THE SHORTEST?**

The longest papacy was held by Pius IX, who was in office for
32 years, and the shortest papacy was held by Stephen II, who
was in office for one day before succumbing to an apoplexy.

THE APOSTOLIC PALACE

The Apostolic Palace contains both your official residence
and your main office. The public apartment of the pontiff
is on the third floor while your private dwelling is on the
fourth floor, facing St. Peter's Square. Take your time getting
to know the palace. Only slightly smaller than the Dalai Lama's
(unoccupied) palace in Tibet, it is one of the biggest such
palaces in the world. With more than 1,400 rooms, 1,000 stair-
cases, and 12,500 windows, it can be a challenge to navigate.

❖ Your private apartment has seven big rooms in addition
to a roof garden, living quarters for your domestic staff,
a large dining room, and your study, which holds your
desk and office space.

❖ It is largely up to you to decide how to furnish your new
living space. Some popes have appointed their living
quarters like a presidential suite, while others have opted
for a more minimalist approach. There is a large, marble
bathroom, however, so even if you opt for spare furnishings, you will still be able to bathe in elegance.

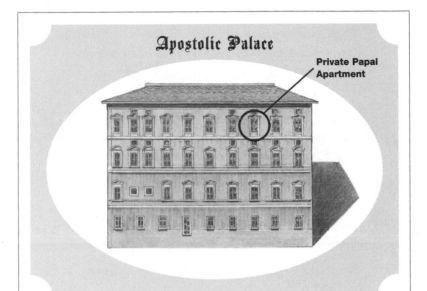

Apostolic Palace

Private Papal Apartment

＊ A chapel in your private apartment seats up to 40, in rows of four behind your bronze chair (designed by Rudelli), which faces the altar, rather than the assembled crowd.

＊ Your public apartment, where you greet many of your important visitors and dignitaries, contains a number of large, ornate rooms, such as the Clementine Hall, which is used for grand occasions and the receiving of aristocracy; Consistory Hall, where you might meet lesser dignitaries; and the Hall of the Popes, which has a giant sculpture of Boniface VIII. For huge crowds, you can use the Hall of General Audiences, which has a papal throne at the base of Pericle Fazzini's towering, bronze Christ sculpture.

* The papal library is also on the third floor and it is where the televised meetings of foreign leaders often take place, from Yasser Arafat to the Dalai Lama. The massive bookshelves contain bibles from different centuries and in many different languages as well as the complete papal encyclicals.

* After the assassination attempt on JP II in 1981, bulletproof glass was installed along your private terrace and in the third-floor window that you use to address the crowd in St. Peter's Square.

* The palace is also home to several of your top cardinals, who have apartments elsewhere in the complex.

* The Apostolic Bank is tucked away in a small tower near the East Façade.

 ### Frequently Asked Questions
WHAT IS AN ANTIPOPE?
An antipope is someone who lays false claim to the title of pope. Usually, an antipope would confirm himself and assume papal duties in direct defiance of the true pope of the time. The last such impostor was Felix V (1440–49).

 ### Frequently Asked Questions
WHAT IF I DON'T LIKE MY QUARTERS?
If you don't like the furnishings in your apartment, you may refashion your quarters as you see fit.

For Your Holiness's Information

PAPAL RENOVATIONS

Some of your predecessors have had very strong ideas about what they wanted in the papal apartment.

---

* The papal residence was initially built for Innocent III in 1198. The first major renovation of the papal living quarters began in 1503, when Julius II decided he wanted rooms above where the previous pope, Alexander VI, had lived.

* In 1508, Julius II hired Raphael to decorate the new papal apartment. It took the artist almost 10 years to complete his work. The results were so spectacular, the subsequent pope, Leo X, made him the chief architect of St. Peter's Basilica.

* Pius XI gave the papal apartment a complete makeover. He added plumbing, an electric kitchen, and the papal elevator, bringing it up to the modern standards of the 1920s.

* Pius XII, a very formal pope, kept a pontifical throne in the cab of his elevator.

* Paul VI redecorated for the modern age, taking out many of the older tapestries, baroque art, and ornate clocks. He replaced them with modern paintings and medieval statues and had the walls repainted in brighter colors. He was also the pontiff who had the upper terrace built, so that he would not have to go down to the Vatican Gardens for a little greenery.

Frequently Asked Questions
WHAT IF THERE'S A FIRE?

There hasn't been a fire in the palace for more than a century, but just in case, the VC maintains a 20-man fire department. The brown-uniformed firemen and their three fire trucks and one hook-and-ladder are on call 24 hours a day.

Frequently Asked Questions
HAVE ALL THE POPES LIVED IN THE PALACE?

No. Popes didn't start residing in the Vatican until the thirteenth century. Before that, they lived in the palace that adjoins the Basilica of St. John Lateran, on the southeast edge of Rome.

Frequently Asked Questions
WHAT IS THERE TO EAT AROUND HERE?

A team of five nuns provides you with your meals, and you can dictate to them precisely what you would like on your menu. For example, JP II was very fond of the comfort food he enjoyed as a child in Poland. He regularly dined on freshly made pierogi and a hot bowl of zurek (potato soup), followed up by sweet babka for dessert. You can also find an espresso machine in almost any office of the Vatican. Many of your dairy products and much of your fresh produce come from your country summer haven, Castel Gandolfo.

Frequently Asked Questions

CAN I GO OUT TO EAT?

While cardinals and bishops can often be found eating in some of Rome's finest restaurants, it is far more rare for the pontiff to eat out. Obvious security issues would have to be dealt with before you could leave the confines of the Vatican and eat in a public restaurant. If you choose to dine in Rome, however, here are some nearby options:

✤ **Il Mozzicone** (Borgo Pio 180; phone 06 686 1500). Known for excellent, traditional Roman fare, such as fettuccine al ragu.

✤ **Velando** (Borgo V. Horio 26; phone 06 6880 9955). Long a favorite of cardinals, Velando features nouveau Italian cuisine with such nontraditional dishes as wild strawberry risotto and frog and vegetable strudel.

✤ **Taverna Angelica** (Piazza Amerigo Capponi 6; phone 06 687 4514). Seafood is their specialty, from smoked fish to eel. They also offer a wide selection of cheeses.

THE PAPAL WARDROBE

Your day-to-day wardrobe depends on your schedule. When conducting business out of the public's eye, you may dress more informally, but for your religious ceremonies you will be required to wear your formal vestments.

Papal Wardrobe

Mozzetta

Fanon

Pallium

Alb

Cappa

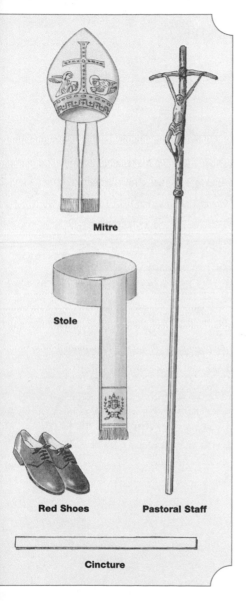

Mitre

Stole

Red Shoes

Pastoral Staff

Cincture

INFORMAL OUTFIT

White trousers
Collarless white shirt
Clerical collar
White skullcap
(*see Papal Hats, on page 26*)
White robe
(called a *simar*) with a sash
Red shoes or sandals

FORMAL VESTMENTS

Amice: a rectangular piece of white linen that covers your neck
Alb: a long white robe
Cincture: a ropelike belt
Stole: a long, scarflike strip of fabric worn over the alb
Mozzetta: a short red cape
Fanon: a double mozzetta, consisting of two pieces of white silk, specifically worn for pontifical mass
Pallium: a collar of white wool, embroidered with six black crosses and worn over the shoulders
Red shoes

For Your Holiness's Information

PAPAL HATS

According to tradition, you will almost always wear at least a zucchetto in public. For more formal occasions, you have several other possibilities.

Zucchetto (skullcap): Worn during more informal events, the small round cap comes from the age-old practice of clerics shaving the middle of their heads to form a patch known as a tonsure.

Mitre: Based on late Roman headgear, it's essentially a cloth crown, with two points, or horns, said to represent both the Old and New Testaments. It is used for more formal ceremonies.

Papal Tiara: The three-tiered crown (studded with jewels and ornamentation), along with the entire coronation ceremony, was renounced by Paul VI, in 1964, who wanted his papacy to be as humble as possible. In place of the regal-like coronation was a far more subdued celebration. John Paul I and JP II followed Paul VI's example and also refused to wear the crown, but you may reinstate its use if you wish.

THE PAPAL TAILORS

Three sets of papal garments in small, medium, and large were made ahead of time before you were selected as the new pope. You should have the garments adjusted as soon as possible. Your official tailor is the small Ditta A. Gammarelli shop situated in downtown Rome, right across the Tiber River from the Vatican. There, tailors work feverishly to hand-make each piece of your wardrobe. For your comfort, every effort is made to use light fabrics, which will help keep you cool during the hottest months of the summer.

Frequently Asked Questions
WHO DOES MY LAUNDRY?
Five black-robed nuns, appointed by you when you first assumed the papacy, take care of your meals and your laundry.

Frequently Asked Questions
WHY DOES EVERYONE KISS MY RING?
The kissing of the pontifical ring is considered an act of respect, showing followers' obedience to the laws and governance of the church.

Essential Papal Knowledge

THE PAPAL SYMBOLS

✤ **Pectoral Cross (across chest):** Usually six inches tall, the cross is worn on a chain around your neck and rests just over your heart.

✤ **Fisherman's Ring:** The reference is to St. Peter, who, among other things, was a fisherman. The ring itself is gold with a precious gem set on it. You wear this at all times.

THE PAPAL RING

✤ Unique to each pope and broken and destroyed upon that pope's demise.

✤ Made of gold.

✤ The image on the ring is of St. Peter in a boat, fishing, with your papal name around the perimeter.

✤ Generally, it is worn on the fourth finger of your left hand.

✤ Until 1842, it was used as a signet to seal all official papal documents.

The Papal Seal

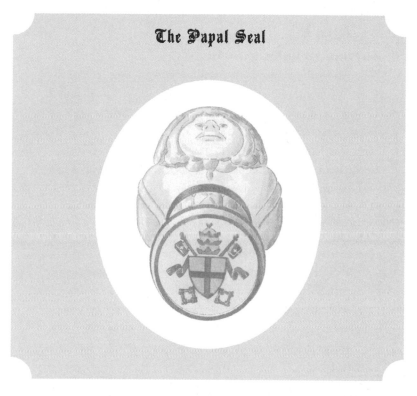

❖ **Papal Seal:** A steel seal that you will use on important text and correspondence. Along with your ring, the seal will be destroyed upon your death, before the next conclave begins.

❖ **Pastoral Staff:** This symbolizes your role as the shepherd of your people. Bishops also have one, but yours is topped with a crucifix.

Essential Papal Knowledge
GETTING TO KNOW VATICAN CITY

The Apostolic Palace is just one of many places in Vatican City (VC) with which you will need to become acquainted. Despite its limited size, the VC offers its citizens a wide range of amenities.

* **Vatican Historic Museum:** Surprisingly, it displays artifacts and mementos from the papacy's military efforts. It includes an arsenal of weapons, from ancient Venetian sabers to Remington muskets.

* **Pontifical Pharmacy:** Just past the Gate of St. Anne's, the pharmacy has many different medicines unavailable in other Italian drugstores. It fills almost 6,000 prescriptions a month, but it doesn't carry any magazines, greeting cards, or batteries. However, it does offer toothpaste, deodorant, and a full line of other personal cosmetics.

* **Vatican Railroad:** Perhaps the shortest line in the world, the railroad covers 2,600 feet and doesn't follow a strict schedule. However, it does have links with the Italian railway system, and the special papal coaches sport a kitchen, balcony, and sleeping quarters.

* **Vatican Library:** Contains more than one million books in addition to 100,000 maps and manuscripts. You are welcome to check out any book for as long as you like.

* **Supermarket:** There is but one, and you will need to bring a DIRESCO (Office of Economic Services)

For Your Holiness's Information
VC INFORMATION AND TRIVIA

Size: 108 acres

Population: 1,100 full-time residents, of which approximately 95% are male. There is no birth rate.

Official Language: Latin

ATMs: The VC's cash dispensers are the only such machines in the world whose principal screen language is in Latin.

Time Zone: CET (Central European Time)

International Telephone Prefix: +39-06

There are no traffic lights.

VC citizens pay no Italian taxes, even if they live in Rome.

It takes about an hour to go all the way around the city, walking along the walls of the VC.

Pet dogs of VC citizens must be registered and kept on a leash at all times.

Planes are not permitted to fly over VC airspace.

identification card in order to make use of the store. Prices are significantly lower here than in the rest of Rome, which makes it very popular among distant family members of the people who can legally buy items at the facility. Known as the Annona (Latin for "gathering of provisions"), it is located on Via San Giovanni di Dio, just behind the pharmacy. Hours of operation are 7 A.M. to 6 P.M. during the week, and until noon on Saturday.

❄ **Vatican Department Store:** Recently relocated to the VC's former train station, the department store has a wide-ranging array of merchandise that stretches from high-end items like big-screen TVs and $1,000 watches all the way down to cartons of tax-free cigarettes, which are anywhere from 20%–40% cheaper than outside the VC.

❄ **Post Office:** Dating back to the fourteenth century, the post office is able to turn a profit, largely by selling commemorative papal stamps. It handles more than eight million letters and cards a year and has a reputation for running far more smoothly than the standard Italian postal service.

❄ **Gas Station:** There are several, but the station just south of St. Peter's is the most popular. Nontaxed VC gas is about 30% cheaper than in the rest of Italy. Only people with special VC permits are allowed to fill up.

⁕ **St. Peter's Basilica:** Covering nearly 430,000 square feet (or enough room for six football fields), it is the largest church in Christendom. Ten million visitors flock to St. Peter's every year to catch a glimpse of any one of the Basilica's 430 statues and 40 different altars. Underneath the Basilica there is actually another church altogether: the Sacred Grottos of the Vatican, also known as the Tomb of the Popes.

For Your Holiness's Information
VC CITIZENSHIP

Citizenship is not granted casually. In 2003, of the 1,100 full-time residents, only half were official citizens, including some 61 cardinals and all 100 members of the Swiss Guard, although any visiting cardinal is granted immediate citizenship. Apart from them, only the highest-ranking church officials on your staff are granted citizenship. Interestingly, all VC passports are diplomatic—all residents are considered diplomats for the church. Other residents live within the confines of the VC, but their access to the VC stores and shops is somewhat limited. Notably, all VC citizens are considered to have dual citizenship along with their original home countries. The rest of the 3,000 people who make up the city's workforce live outside the VC limits, in Rome.

The Vatican Euro

Front

Back

Frequently Asked Questions

WHAT CURRENCY IS USED IN THE VC?

The official VC currency is the euro of the Vatican. Many of the VC coins have a visage of the pope on them.

Frequently Asked Questions

WHAT IS THE EXCHANGE RATE?

The euro of the Vatican is equivalent to the standard euro.

Frequently Asked Questions

DOES THE VC HAVE A JAIL?

The VC has two small jail cells, but any criminal sentenced to prison is quickly transferred to the Italian prison system.

Frequently Asked Questions

WHAT IF I NEED A DOCTOR?

If you need medical attention, your own personal physician is available any time you desire. You also have your choice of specialists, should the need arise. For serious medical conditions, you would probably be transferred out of the VC to one of Rome's fully equipped hospitals. You can tell your security handlers in advance which hospital you would prefer to be taken to in times of dire need, as JP II did before he was shot.

CHAPTER II

Getting Down to Work

The papacy is one of the world's oldest and most prestigious jobs, but it requires you to wake up early and work all through the day and evening—with a break for the midafternoon siesta, which is as much a tradition in the Vatican as it is throughout the rest of Italy. Every day you will face a busy schedule of meetings, special audiences, and paperwork, as you juggle the worldwide affairs of the church with the nitty-gritty of running the Vatican itself. Fortunately, you work in world-class facilities and a loyal staff of expert subordinates stands ready to help you keep on top of things. Your office, right next to your living quarters, is host to a constant flow of visitors, from your personal secretaries to high-ranking cardinals.

Essential Papal Knowledge

YOUR JOB DESCRIPTION

Your job description can be broken down into a number of different (and often overlapping) roles:

- **Vicar of Christ:** You are Christ's representative on Earth, the keeper of the faith for the church.

- **Pontifex Maximus:** You are the supreme pontiff of the church. This gives you the last word on all matters of faith, ethics, and discipline within the organization. The members of the church consider your word in matters of faith and morality infallible. You can appoint cardinals and archbishops and bishops as you see fit. You can discipline and silence members of the church who perform heresy, as you define it. You also write and release periodic encyclicals to bring attention to particular philosophies you espouse. Your main goal as leader of the church is to bring coherence and unity to believers.

- **Bishop of Rome:** You oversee the pastoral needs of the city's faithful. Additionally, as the top bishop, you lead by example for bishops all over the world. You have the authority to teach and discipline all the other members of the clergy.

- **Head of State:** You lead the Vatican city-state. The VC has full diplomatic relations with most other countries and maintains a permanent observer status at the U.N. The president of the *governatorate,* who acts as mayor of the VC, oversees much of the VC's everyday business—but he answers directly to you.

✢ **Outspoken Mouthpiece of the Values of the Church:**
Since JP II, who transformed his papacy into a global pulpit, you are expected to speak as a voice of conscience, articulating the needs of the world's poor and powerless and calling out despotic world leaders and regimes.

Essential Papal Knowledge

YOUR TITLES

You are now officially the Bishop of Rome, Vicar of Jesus Christ, Successor to the Prince of the Apostles, Supreme Pontiff of the Universal Church, Patriarch of the West, Primate of Italy, Archbishop and Metropolitan of the Province of Rome, Sovereign of the Vatican City, and Servant of the Servants of God.

Frequently Asked Questions

YOUR WORK SPACE

The decoration of your office space is, like the rest of your apartment, largely up to you. As a standard, you have a desk, chair, phone, and basic reception furniture for official visitors and staff. JP II liked to keep a table for photo books he was particularly taken with so that visitors would have something to do while waiting for their pontifical appointment.

THE PAPAL THRONE

The traditional papal throne, called the *sedia gestatoria*, is used on short trips to raise the pontiff above the crowd. This silk-lined armchair is connected to a *suppedaneum*, which, when hoisted onto the shoulders of 12 footmen, carries you aloft. The portable throne was rarely used by John Paul I and his successor, JP II—both preferred walking among their constituents. A magnificent ornate bronze throne, designed by Bernini, resides at St. Peter's but isn't used as a conveyance.

 Frequently Asked Questions

WHERE DO I GO IN AN EMERGENCY?
TO THE CATACOMBS?

In case of attack, there is no panic room per se, but there are places deep underground where you would be taken.

* **The original papal escape shelter** was the Castel Sant'Angelo, built on the banks of the Tiber in the middle of Rome. It was first built as a mausoleum for Emperor Hadrian between A.D. 123 and 139 and acquired by the church in 1377. The Vatican reworked the building to make it impregnable so the pope would have a safe place to run to in case of crisis. A covered passageway known as the Passetto del Borgo connected the Vatican to the Castel, where there was a separate well-appointed papal apartment as well as a giant safe for all the papal treasures.

The Papal Throne

- ❄ **The Vatican catacombs** consist of an intricate labyrinth of underground tunnels beneath Rome. It is where many early Christians and Jews were buried centuries ago. During the persecutions, in the middle of the fourth century, the catacombs became shrines to the martyrs. In a crisis situation, while it's not inconceivable you might use the catacombs as a hiding place, it is unlikely.

- ❄ **The Vatican Library** uses a high-security underground vault to house some of the Vatican's most precious relics and papers. This vault, dedicated by JP II in the mid-1980s, is one of the more likely places you might be sequestered in an emergency.

Frequently Asked Questions

CAN I DISPLAY HISTORIC ART FROM THE VATICAN VAULTS IN MY OFFICE?

You may redecorate the papal office in any manner you choose, and the giant warehouse of art stored in the Apostolic Palace is available for your personal use.

Essential Papal Knowledge

THE PAPAL SCHEDULE

- ❄ **Your day will start** around 5:30 A.M., whereupon you will either dress yourself or have your papal valet assist you.

- ❄ **After your prayers** in your private chapel, you will conduct mass for your immediate staff and a few privileged guests.

✥ **Breakfast** is at approximately 8 A.M. There will be excellent Italian coffee waiting for you, in addition to whatever daily spread you request. JP II was very fond of breakfast kielbasa, while Benedict XIII was so fond of a particular egg dish that it was named after him back in the eighteenth century.

✥ **Your daily schedule** includes regular meetings with a great number of bishops, who come to the palace from all over the world for their five-year *ad limina* visits, during which they must spend time in the VC and gain an audience with you. You also have regular meetings with the priests of your own diocese in Rome.

✥ **Lunch** is around noon and is usually a working affair, with further meetings with members of the Curia (the bureaucracy administering the affairs of the church). The menu is again at your request, but pasta is not uncommon.

✥ **Meetings with various luminaries** and dignitaries occur throughout the day. Each meeting will likely involve a photo op.

✥ **The hours from roughly 2 to 4 P.M.** are set aside for a siesta, the traditional Italian postlunch resting time. You may choose to work through the siesta hours, as JP II did, but you'll find that most of your staff will not join you.

✥ **Dinner** is around 6 P.M. You can choose to either dine by yourself, as Pius XII often did, or dine with guests, as both John Paul I and JP II preferred.

✥ **Bedtime** is around 11 P.M. This is your chance to do some light reading before retiring to your chambers.

THE VATICAN GARDENS

The Vatican Gardens are one of the best-kept secrets in the world, unsurpassed in beauty by any of the other grand gardens in Europe. The gardens are a place to unwind and spend some time in quiet reflection.

---

* The gardens are meticulously manicured and maintained by a full-time staff of 20 groundskeepers.

* There are many fountains, but the most spectacular is the seventeenth-century Fountain of the Galera (Galleon Fountain), which features a scale model of an Italian cruiser with some 16 cannons "firing" water.

* The gardens have been in existence since 1280, when Nicholas III had a small vegetable garden created. The vegetable garden still provides fresh produce for your consumption.

* The modern gardens were mostly created under Leo XIII in the late nineteenth century.

* In addition to the fountains, the gardens contain a small, neatly manicured forest, known as the Boschetto, as well as many English-style flowerbeds and several neatly manicured European-style gardens.

Fountain of the Galera

Frequently Asked Questions

HOW DO I GET MAIL?

Your mailing address:
His Holiness [Papal Name]
Apostolic Palace
00120 Vatican City-State, EUROPE

Frequently Asked Questions

WILL I HAVE ANY HELP ANSWERING MY MAIL?

One member of the five-nun team that serves as your personal staff (the nuns also make your meals and do your laundry) will be assigned to help you wade through your daily correspondence. You can expect to receive some 800 pounds of mail every day.

Frequently Asked Questions

WHAT NAME DO I USE TO SIGN PAPERS?

You will sign official documents using your Latin papal name. For personal correspondence with old friends, you may use your discretion, though many popes have opted to simply use their papal name in all cases. Traditionally, all popes sign documents with a "p. p." after their name, which stands for "Pastor Pastorum" (Shepherd of Shepherds).

Frequently Asked Questions

DO I HAVE INTERNET ACCESS? HOW DO I GET NEWS?

There is a Vatican Web site (http://www.vatican.va/), as well as a papal e-mail address, which would be your papal name followed by @vatican.va. As far as the news goes, a team of priests prepares a daily digest of information about events and happenings all over the world. It's about 20 pages long and is handed to you by 10:00 in the morning each day.

Frequently Asked Questions

IS THERE A VATICAN NEWSPAPER?

The official Vatican newspaper is the daily *L'Osservatore Romano*, started in 1861, which has a circulation of 60,000. There is also the quarterly *Acta Apostolicae Sedis*, but it only publishes official church documents and legislation.

Frequently Asked Questions

HOW DO I MAKE PHONE CALLS?

The VC has one of the best phone systems in the world, manned by a team of telephone operators from the Six Brothers of the Don Orione Society, which flawlessly handles more than 18,000 calls a day. There are also more telephones in the VC per capita than anywhere else in the world. In order to call out of the VC, you must first dial a 2.

CHAPTER III

Getting to Know Your Staff

✤

You have an extraordinary amount of work to accomplish, and, as CEO of an enormously complex institution, you have to set the standards and practices for everyone else to follow. Thankfully, a small but extremely dedicated personal staff will help you keep track of all your responsibilities. You preside over two separate bureaucracies—one, the Curia, runs the worldwide affairs of the Catholic Church, and the other, the Pontifical Commission, runs the VC. Both governing bodies run lean—the total number of workers doesn't exceed 3,000, which amounts to one employee for every 350,000 church members.

YOUR PERSONAL STAFF

✣ **Secretaries:** Two monsignors act as your full-time secretaries, under the supervision of your private papal secretary. They are there to help you keep on schedule through the confusing tangle of your daily business. They greet your incoming guests and hold an iron grip on your appointments, controlling other peoples' access to you. They also invite the special guests you designate to attend your private morning mass.

✣ **Papal Private Secretary:** Responsible for overseeing your small secretarial staff. The position is considered one of the most powerful in the VC because of its nearly constant contact with you. In the past, some papal secretaries have challenged even the cardinal secretary of state in their importance and indispensability.

✣ **Five nuns** tend to your daily needs, cooking your meals, writing your dictated correspondence, doing your laundry, and cleaning the papal apartment.

✣ **Cardinal Camerlengo (Chamberlain):** The cardinal camerlengo's principal duties begin when you die. It is his duty to inform the other cardinals of your death, and he takes charge of your body and worldly possessions. He removes and destroys your fisherman's ring and seals your apartment until the next pontiff is elected. He is also in charge of the church during the "vacant see" until the next pontiff is elected.

Essential Papal Knowledge

THE ROMAN CURIA

The Curia is a vast bureaucracy consisting of innumerable offices, commissions, committees, congregations, and tribunals. You will very likely not have much interaction with most of them. However, it is vital that you know well the offices and positions that will deal directly with you.

* **Secretariat of State:** The Secretariat sits atop the flow chart, just under you in terms of authority. It coordinates all the departments within the Vatican and filters the major issues and decisions before they get to you. It is divided into two entities, the Section for General Affairs and the Section for Relation of States.

* **Cardinal Secretary of State:** The head of the Secretariat, he acts as your point person on important papal matters. He is, essentially, the prime minister of the church. He represents the Vatican in international matters, receives visiting dignitaries, and accompanies you when you travel. Unlike most of the other higher-ups in the Vatican, he is not subject to a five-year term of office, although he does immediately lose his job when you die.

* **The Section for General Affairs:** Handles most of the internal affairs of the church and ranks in importance just under the Secretariat of State. Among other functions, the Section is responsible for issuing papal texts and preparing your public speeches. For these purposes, the body is broken up into eight language-based departments: English, French, German, Italian, Latin, Polish, Portuguese,

and Spanish. The Section is also responsible for the more than 200 papal diplomats stationed around the world.

- ✣ *Il Sostituto* **(The Substitute):** The *sostituto* presides over the Section for General Affairs. Held by an archbishop, it is considered the Number-two post, just under the cardinal secretary of state. The *sostituto* is, essentially, your chief of staff, helping to smooth out the daily operations of the office and deciding which issues you need to deal with.

- ✣ **The Section for Relation of States:** Oversees the Vatican's diplomatic relations with foreign governments and international organizations (even though it doesn't directly oversee the diplomats themselves). It is also responsible for the nomination of new bishops and the creation of new dioceses.

- ✣ **The Secretary for Relations of States:** Heads the second branch of the Secretariat, but his power is considered beneath the cardinal secretary of state and the *sostituto*.

Essential Papal Knowledge

THE PONTIFICAL COMMISSION

Even though part of your job description includes the governance of the Vatican City-State, you delegate most of this authority to other church officials.

- ✣ **The Pontifical Commission** comprises five cardinals who are led by the president of the *governatorate* of the VC (essentially, the mayor).

✤ **The president of the *governatorate*** maintains the city's infrastructure and oversees all the city services, as well as the VC's $190 million budget. The VC takes in money primarily through the issuance of papal coins and stamps and, more recently, from several shops and stores, including an extremely lucrative gas station.

Frequently Asked Questions

HOW SHOULD PEOPLE ADDRESS ME?

You have many appellations, but in direct contact everyone should refer to you as "Your Holiness."

Frequently Asked Questions

WHAT IS PETER'S PENCE?

Peter's Pence is another major source of income for the Vatican. The term refers to the annual contributions from church members all over the world, usually collected on the last Sunday in June. The total amount ranges from about $25 million to $35 million each year.

Frequently Asked Questions

I RUN AN INDEPENDENT STATE. DO I ALSO HAVE AN ARMY?

Under international law, the Vatican could form a navy and an air force, but as it stands now, you have neither. The Swiss Guards are the closest thing you have to a military force.

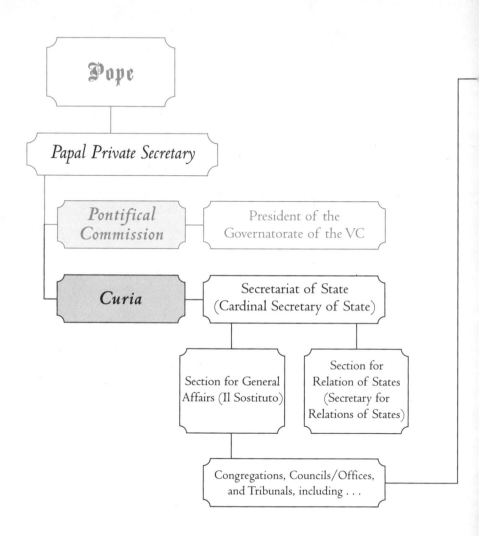

Congregations:

Congregation for the Doctrine of the Faith: Determines official teachings and doctrine of the church. Leads investigations against any clergy who deviate and also manages legal responsibility for major crimes involving priests.

Congregation for the Causes of Saints: Reviews nominees for beatification and canonization.

Congregation for Bishops: Supervises appointment and organization of bishops.

Congregation for Clergy: Oversees all clerical discipline and creation of clergy members.

Congregation for Catholic Education: Supervises all Catholic schools and universities.

Councils/Offices:

Pontifical Council for Laity: Coordinates Christian life among the layperson members of the church.

Pontifical Council for the Family: Promotes and protects the church's doctrine on family.

Pontifical Council for Justice and Peace: Promotes the church's official social doctrines, in particular with respect to war, the environment, and economic development of underprivileged countries.

Pontifical Council for Culture: Promotes the church's worldwide vision of mass communications, including newspapers, TV, radio, and the Internet.

Office of the Liturgical Celebrations of the Supreme Pontiff: Organizes pontifical liturgies and ceremonies, including ceremonies performed in other countries when you travel.

Tribunals:

Apostolic Penitentiary: Handles various delicate workings of the church, including the "sphere of internal conscience," wherein sins and confession within the clergy are addressed. Also oversees religious disputes, including the validation and invalidation of marriages.

Roman Rota: Main judicial office of the Vatican. Acts as an appeals court for decisions and decrees made by local church offices around the world. Also oversees, in conjunction with the Apostolic Penitentiary, requests for formal marriage annulments.

Supreme Tribunal of the Apostolic Signatura: Highest court of appeals in the church.

Frequently Asked Questions

HOW MANY PEOPLE WORK FOR ME IN THE VC?

You have approximately 3,500 full-time employees under you, of which roughly 1,500 are clergy. Of the total 3,500, two-thirds work for the Holy See and one-third work for the VC.

For Your Holiness's Information

CATHOLIC STATS

Increase in number of Catholics from 1978 to 2000:
288 million

Catholics as a percentage of world population:
Approximately 17%–18%, unchanged since 1970

Catholics as percentages of regional populations:
62.4% of the Americas, 40.5% of Europe, 26.8% of Oceania, 16.5% of Africa, and 3% of Asia

Countries with highest percentage of Catholics: The Vatican (100%), San Marino (99.83%), Saint Pierre (99.36%), Wallis and Futuna Islands (99.02%), Italy (97.20%)

U.S. state with highest percentage of Catholic observance: Rhode Island, at 63%

U.S. state with most Catholics: New York, with more than 7 million

U.S. county with the highest percentage of Catholics:
Kenedy, Texas, at 95.65%

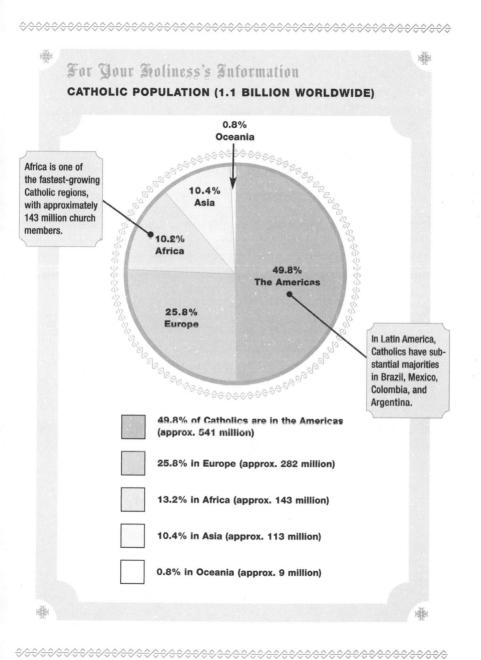

For Your Holiness's Information

CATHOLIC POPULATION (1.1 BILLION WORLDWIDE)

0.8%
Oceania

10.4%
Asia

Africa is one of the fastest-growing Catholic regions, with approximately 143 million church members.

10.2%
Africa

49.8%
The Americas

25.8%
Europe

In Latin America, Catholics have substantial majorities in Brazil, Mexico, Colombia, and Argentina.

49.8% of Catholics are in the Americas (approx. 541 million)

25.8% in Europe (approx. 282 million)

13.2% in Africa (approx. 143 million)

10.4% in Asia (approx. 113 million)

0.8% in Oceania (approx. 9 million)

IDENTIFYING YOUR CLERGY

The church's clergy are organized in a strict hierarchy. Each rank carries with it special privileges of dress and title. Fortunately, you will be able to recognize the various ranks of the officials reporting to you by the different vestments they wear.

- **Cardinals (population, 178):** They wear red robes and hats (red symbolizes the blood they are willing to spill for the church) and, when spoken to, are referred to as "Your Eminence." You appoint them and they, in turn, will elect the next pope.

- **Bishops/Archbishops (approximate population, 4,000):** Most often, they wear a black cassock with red piping or a purple cassock for church functions. They are referred to as "Your Excellency." Bishops are also appointed by you.

- **Priests (approximate population, 400,000):** Priests commonly wear black. They assist their bishops with the daily running of a given church. They are referred to as "Father." On rare occasions, a priest will be given a special blessing and is thenceforth referred to as "Monsignor."

Your Clergy

Cardinal

Priest

Bishop

CHAPTER IV

Rituals, Ceremonies, and Public Appearances

*

Much of your day is filled with symbolic activities.
Sunday masses are perhaps the most well known
of your regular public appearances, but there are
many others. You are required to attend the ceremonies of all the special holy days of the church,
including saints' and martyrs' days. You will also
spend a lot of time meeting with dignitaries and
representatives from other countries, and, following
the example of JP II, you will have to go out into
the world and evangelize on behalf of the church,
spreading the word and meeting up with the multi-
tude of church followers all over the world.

Essential Papal Knowledge

MASS

The religious service you will most often perform is mass in St. Peter's Square on Sunday mornings.

* **Beginning:** Mass starts with an entrance hymn, followed by a few short penitential rites and then the Gospel, in which the entire audience participates.

* **Middle:** The offertory, the offering of bread and wine to God, is performed, followed by the washing of hands, the prayers, and thanks and ending in Sanctus (a hymn). Then there is the long canon prayer, starting with the prayers for the living, followed by the consecration of bread and wine, the raising of the host and chalice for the crowd to see, and the prayers for the dead.

* **End:** This starts with the Lord's Prayer, then the breaking of the host (after which a piece is placed in the chalice), followed by the kiss of peace, the Agnus Dei, and communion. The service ends with the ablution of vessels, post-communion prayers, the dismissal, and, finally, the blessing.

Frequently Asked Questions

HOW DO I DISTRIBUTE COMMUNION TO 40,000 PEOPLE?

Fortunately, you are not required to distribute communion to all the attendees after you bless them. There will be a small, select group to whom you will personally distribute communion while the rest will be served by a huge contingent of priests, bishops, and cardinals.

PAPAL MASS NOTES

✤ Approximately four to five million people attended a mass JP II held in the Philippines in 1995, the largest modern papal mass.

✤ Arguably, the smallest modern papal mass was attended by just 200 people, who braved the elements for an outdoor mass JP II gave in the Nordic countries in 1989.

✤ In perhaps the largest U.S. indoor gathering ever, 104,000 people packed into the Edward Jones Dome and five adjoining exhibit halls in the America's Center complex in St. Louis, Missouri, for a mass JP II gave in 1999.

✤ Perhaps the most vexing mass JP II ever attempted was an outdoor ceremony in Miami in 1987. Hundreds of thousands of people came to take part, but torrential rain forced the mass to end early. Amid gale-force winds, JP II was whisked away from the altar and taken, soaking wet, to a special trailer where he was toweled off. Running late, he only had time to eat part of a fruit cocktail before he was taken back to the Miami airport. Years later, he referred to the incident simply as "Miami, the rain."

✤ A single communion wafer blessed by JP II back in 1998 was sold on eBay for $2,000, but because of public outcry the transaction was never completed and the owner withdrew the item from bidding.

For Your Holiness's Information

EASTER MASS

Easter, the most holy and celebratory day in the Catholic calendar, requires a special four-day ceremony. Thousands of followers come to Rome to celebrate with the church. This is a particularly busy 96-hour schedule for you, so you should plan accordingly.

HOLY THURSDAY

Morning: At St. Peter's Basilica, preside over a special mass that blesses the holy oils.

EVENING: Lead the Mass of the Lord's Supper in St. Peter's. Wash the feet of 12 priests, re-creating the act of Christ during the Last Supper.

GOOD FRIDAY

Afternoon: Hold a small service in St. Peter's, as no mass is performed on this day of mourning. During the service, an account of Christ's death is sung and participants kiss the cross before they receive communion.

Evening: Lead the procession of the 14 Stations of the Cross at the Coliseum, commemorating the Passion. At each station, you read a meditation before moving on to the next.

HOLY SATURDAY

Late evening: You celebrate mass at St. Peter's.

EASTER SUNDAY

Mass is celebrated in St. Peter's Square. Expect an audience of between 40,000 and 150,000 people and possibly many more. After this mass, deliver your blessing, *Urbi et orbi* (*see* A Latin Primer, *page 69*), from a balcony at St. Peter's.

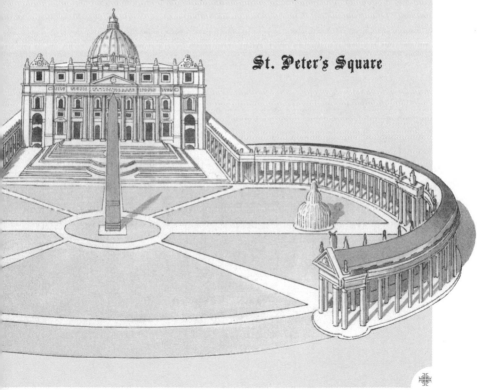

St. Peter's Square

Essential Papal Knowledge

SPECIAL OCCASIONS ON THE CATHOLIC CALENDAR

Here are some highlights from the special days to observe on the Catholic calendar. Be sure to note that some of the dates are not set fast each year.

January 1: The Solemnity of Mary, Mother of God

January 28: St. Thomas Aquinas Memorial

February: Ash Wednesday/Lent

February 22: Feast of the Chair of St. Peter

March/April: Sixth Week of Easter

April 7: St. John the Baptist Memorial

April 25: Feast of St. Mark

May 2: St. Athanasius Memorial

May 5: The Solemnity of the Ascension of the Lord

May 15: Feast of Pentecost

JANUARY						
S	M	T	W	T	F	S
						1
2	3	4	5	6	7	8
9	10	11	12	13	14	15
16	17	18	19	20	21	22
23	24	25	26	27	28	29
30	31					

FEBRUARY						
S	M	T	W	T	F	S
		1	2	3	4	5
6	7	8	9	10	11	12
13	14	15	16	17	18	19
20	21	22	23	24	25	26
27	28					

MARCH						
S	M	T	W	T	F	S
		1	2	3	4	5
6	7	8	9	10	11	12
13	14	15	16	17	18	19
20	21	22	23	24	25	26
27	28	29	30	31		

APRIL						
S	M	T	W	T	F	S
					1	2
3	4	5	6	7	8	9
10	11	12	13	14	15	16
17	18	19	20	21	22	23
24	25	26	27	28	29	30

MAY						
S	M	T	W	T	F	S
1	2	3	4	5	6	7
8	9	10	11	12	13	14
15	16	17	18	19	20	21
22	23	24	25	26	27	28
29	30	31				

JUNE						
S	M	T	W	T	F	S
			1	2	3	4
5	6	7	8	9	10	11
12	13	14	15	16	17	18
19	20	21	22	23	24	25
26	27	28	29	30		

July 22: St. Mary Magdalene Memorial

July 25: Feast of St. James

August 15: The Solemnity of the Assumption of the Blessed Virgin Mary

August 24: Feast of St. Bartholomew

September 15: Our Lady of Sorrows Memorial

September 21: Feast of St. Matthew

October 4: St. Francis Memorial

October 17: St. Ignatius Memorial

October 18: Feast of St. Luke

November/December: Advent

November 1: All Saints' Day

November 2: All Souls' Day

November 30: Feast of St. Andrew

December 3: St. Francis Xavier Memorial

December 8: The Solemnity of the Immaculate Conception

December 13: St. Lucy Memorial

December 25: The Solemnity of the Nativity

JULY

S	M	T	W	T	F	S
					1	2
3	4	5	6	7	8	9
10	11	12	13	14	15	16
17	18	19	20	21	22	23
24	25	26	27	28	29	30
31						

AUGUST

S	M	T	W	T	F	S
	1	2	3	4	5	6
7	8	9	10	11	12	13
14	15	16	17	18	19	20
21	22	23	24	25	26	27
28	29	30	31			

SEPTEMBER

S	M	T	W	T	F	S
				1	2	3
4	5	6	7	8	9	10
11	12	13	14	15	16	17
18	19	20	21	22	23	24
25	26	27	28	29	30	

OCTOBER

S	M	T	W	T	F	S
						1
2	3	4	5	6	7	8
9	10	11	12	13	14	15
16	17	18	19	20	21	22
23	24	25	26	27	28	29
30	31					

NOVEMBER

S	M	T	W	T	F	S
		1	2	3	4	5
6	7	8	9	10	11	12
13	14	15	16	17	18	19
20	21	22	23	24	25	26
27	28	29	30			

DECEMBER

S	M	T	W	T	F	S
				1	2	3
4	5	6	7	8	9	10
11	12	13	14	15	16	17
18	19	20	21	22	23	24
25	26	27	28	29	30	31

WASHING OF FEET RITUAL

On Holy Thursday, priests everywhere are required to wash 12 peoples' feet in homage to Christ, who washed the feet of the Apostles before the Last Supper. You, in turn, will wash the feet of 12 priests in St. Peter's to continue the tradition of humbleness and humility. JP II also famously kissed the feet of the priests he had just washed, but this is optional.

Pope Kissing the Foot of a Priest

A LATIN PRIMER

A quick brush-up on your conversational language skills, these essential phrases should help get you through your busy day:

Yes = Ita
No = Non
Hello = Salve
Thank you = Gratias
Please = Sis
Good = Bene
Bad = Male
Nice to meet you = Suave est tibi occurere
You haven't aged a bit = Minime senuisti
I am hungry again = Irascor iterum
Let us pray = Permissum nos precor
Rome has spoken, the case is closed = Roma locuta, causa finites
To the city and the world (the pope's traditional blessing) = Urbi et orbi

Essential Papal Knowledge
PAPAL AUDIENCES

Meeting lay members of your church as well as foreign dignitaries is all in a day's work. In fact, popes down through the ages have always made a point of meeting with world leaders and the accomplished artists of their day.

- **Attila the Hun met with Leo I in 452.** No one quite knows the exact conversation, but Attila did leave Italy with his army in tow shortly thereafter.

- **Clark Gable was asked to meet with Pius XII,** known as one of the more dour popes in recent times. Apparently, Pius XII was very fond of Hollywood movies.

- **Novelist Graham Greene had a papal visit with Paul VI** and was told by the enthusiastic pontiff that his work had been much appreciated, even though several of his books had been officially banned by the church.

- **Golfer Sam Snead visited with John XXIII** in hopes of having his putter blessed, as he had been enduring a rough patch on the greens. He thought better of the request after a monsignor at the palace confessed that, despite his piety, his own putting game had also gone south.

Frequently Asked Questions
WHAT'S A GOOD ICEBREAKER?

Breaking the ice and making conversation with a new acquaintance, particularly in a public setting, requires a deft touch. Other than a lightly self-effacing comment, humor can be a tricky way to connect with people. To be on the safe side, you may want to casually inform your guest that he or she is looking well, has lost weight, looks years younger, etc. In politics, as elsewhere, heartfelt flattery is always appreciated. Many public luminaries have learned the trick of memorizing names quickly so that they can promptly establish a personal rapport. Any connection you can make to the guest's home country or city will also be warmly received. If you've had contact with the guest before, asking after his or her family is always a safe bet.

Frequently Asked Questions

WHERE DO DIGNITARIES STAY IN THE VC?

Most visiting dignitaries stay at the Domus Sanctae Marthae (St. Martha's House), which was finished in 1996. Unlike some of the guests' quarters in the Apostolic Palace, which are spare and rustic, this five-story, 107-suite residence offers heat and A/C and visitors can enjoy their own private bathrooms. On the ground floor is an eating hall, with large, elegant round tables. It's still not a five-star hotel, but it's much better than previous housing arrangements.

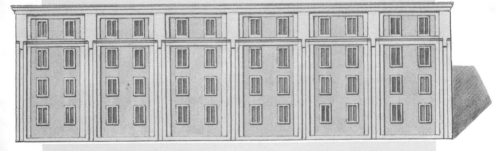

St. Martha's House

Frequently Asked Questions

CAN I SHARE MEALS WITH VISITORS?

Whether or not you share your meals with your visitors is largely up to you. Some popes, Pius XII among them, almost never ate with dignitaries or anyone else. Others, like JP II, took every meal with either staff or special visitors. From a diplomatic point of view, it's always a good idea to break bread with your guests, but that, like many such decisions related to the business of the church, is entirely your call.

Essential Papal Knowledge

HOW TO GREET WORLD LEADERS

You are invested with enormous moral authority, and world leaders who come to meet you will very likely be much more nervous about meeting you than the other way around. So, while it is important to greet your guests in the appropriate manner, they are bound to be too distracted to notice minor deviations in protocol.

✳ **U.S. President:** Greet with a firm handshake. After you've established a rapport, in future meetings you may also clasp the shoulder of the arm you are shaking.

✳ **Malaysian Prime Minister:** A less than firm handshake, followed by a placing of your right hand over your heart.

✳ **Japanese Emperor:** A deep, slow bow from the waist.

✳ **Prime Minister of Laos:** Place your palms together in a prayer-like manner in front of your face or chest.

- ✤ **King of Thailand:** Palms together as with the prime minister of Laos, only add a slow head nod to the gesture.

- ✤ **Prime Minister of England:** A firm handshake.

- ✤ **The Dalai Lama:** Bow your head, making no eye contact.

- ✤ **Queen of England:** Accept her offer of a handshake; do so lightly, while addressing her as "Your Majesty." Do not show her your back, and leave a room only after she does.

 ## Frequently Asked Questions

DO I EVER GIVE PRESS CONFERENCES?

The last several popes have made public statements in the Hall of Benedictions above the portico of St. Peter's. But JP II turned what had previously been a bland opportunity for a standard speech reading into an off-the-cuff, interactive Q&A with the adoring Italian press.

VISITING YOUR (WORLDWIDE) CONGREGATION

To spread the teachings of the church and to maintain the church's influence in the lives of your followers, you will need to spend time among them. As such, you can plan to make several major tours outside the Vatican each year. The most traveled pope was JP II, who visited 129 different countries on 104 official foreign visits in 26 years. (*See Chapter VI for more information about traveling.*)

Frequently Asked Questions

HOW MANY LANGUAGES DO I NEED TO KNOW?
It helps to know as many languages as possible. JP II was fluent in English, French, German, Italian, Latin, Polish, and Russian. Cardinal Giuseppe Mezzofanti, born in 1774, was said to have mastered 39 languages by the time of his death.

For Your Holiness's Information

BIBLE QUOTATIONS
These Bible quotations are basic utility phrases useful for almost any occasion.

You are "Rock," and on this rock I will build My Church and the gates of hell shall not prevail against it. MATTHEW 16:13–20

God blesses those whose hearts are pure, for they will see God. MATTHEW 5:8

Ye cannot serve God and Mammon. MATTHEW 6:24

Love does not delight in evil but rejoices with the truth. I CORINTHIANS 13:6

For what profit is it to a man if he gains the whole world, and loses his own soul? Or what will a man give in exchange for his soul? MATTHEW 16:26

Be not overcome with evil, but overcome evil with good. ROMANS 12:21

Wide is the gate and broad is the way that leadeth to destruction. MATTHEW 7:13

Frequently Asked Questions
DO I HAVE A SPECIAL WAVE?

Your wave serves to raise peoples' spirits. Simply raise your hand, slightly bent at the elbow with your fingers loosely outstretched, and lower it slightly, then raise it again in the same manner. Repeat this gesture as needed.

Papal Wave

Encyclical Letter

Fides
et Ratio

On the Relationship
between
Faith and Reason

John Paul II

CHAPTER V

Special Responsibilities

In addition to the day-to-day business of the papacy and your ceremonial and ritual obligations, you have a number of other important duties. These range from naming new saints and confirming miracles to appointing new cardinals. You also will be expected to write regularly and, through your writings, address pressing church issues and shape official church doctrine. It is also ultimately up to you to enforce church doctrine, and you might be called upon to discipline a member of the church or even excommunicate him or her. Finally, you must oversee the church body that is concerned with exorcisms and the ridding of demons from the innocent souls they've taken possession of.

Essential Papal Knowledge
CREATING SAINTS

Only you can entitle saints, and because your decision to canonize an individual—thereby making him or her a saint—is considered an infallible act, the prestige and credibility of the church is at stake. Whom you choose sends a public signal about the values at the heart of your papacy. The review process is lengthy and involves the work of numerous church officials, but your judgment ultimately determines who is worthy of sainthood.

�֍ The Congregation for the Causes of Saints is the church department tasked with preparing everything necessary for you to be able to evaluate a candidate for sainthood. When they find a worthy enough candidate, submitted by a petitioner from a regional diocese, they present the case to you.

✖ The Congregation is directed by a cardinal, and as many as 150 other church officials contribute to its work.

✖ At any given time, there may be as many as 1,500 candidates awaiting sainthood consideration.

✖ For every candidate, you are presented with a *positio*— the formal, printed argument for granting the nominee sainthood. It includes an extensive biography, summaries of witnesses' accounts, essays discussing the merits of the nominee, and the Congregation's findings concerning the miracles attributed to the candidate.

✤ After reviewing the *positio*, you decide whether you deem the nominee worthy of veneration, beatification, or, if you approve the results on the miracles, canonization.

For Your Holiness's Information
THE ROAD TO SAINTHOOD

Veneration: After a candidate for sainthood has died, you may declare the nominee a person of heroic virtue.

Beatification: This means the nominee is worthy of emulation and a public cult of praise within a given church diocese; henceforth the beatified nominee is referred to as "blessed." In order to be beatified, the nominee must have performed at least one confirmed miracle (*see Confirming Miracles, page 83*).

Canonization: The nominee is granted sainthood and is declared to be in Heaven with God. In addition, his or her cult of praise is spread throughout the church. This nominee will henceforth be referred to as a saint. In order to be canonized, the nominee must have performed at least two confirmed miracles.

FAMOUS SAINTS

St. Peter: One of the apostles, he was the first pope and was appointed by Jesus. He was later killed by the Romans, who either crucified him or, some speculate, threw him to the lions.

St. Nicholas: A bishop who lived in the early fourth century, St. Nicholas was canonized for the miracle he performed by bringing three young children back to life. This helped him become the patron saint of children.

St. Patrick: Born around 373, he is the missionary credited with converting all of Ireland to Catholicism. He started out as a slave in Ireland but was later freed and escaped to France, only to return some 38 years later to evangelize and convert Ireland's lost souls.

St. Francis of Assisi: Born in 1182, St. Francis was imprisoned early in his life by the Perugians, with whom the Assisians were at war. When he was released a year later, he decided to devote his life to the church. Approached by a beggar while passing through Rome, he gave the man his money and his clothes and became a beggar himself as a lesson in humility. Later, he started the Franciscan order, whose adherents dedicate themselves to a life of chastity, poverty, and humble obedience.

St. Joan of Arc: Born in 1412, Joan of Arc started hearing voices at a very early age. The voices told her to reconquer the French kingdom, which at the time had been all but taken over by England. At the age of 17, she was granted a small army, which met with incredible military success, enabling the king of France to retake his throne. Later, she was captured and sold to the British and burned at the stake as a heretic. However, a short while after her death she was exonerated by the church and, five centuries later, canonized.

St. Padre Pio: Said to have received the stigmata in 1918. He was actually blacklisted by the church for several years before a young priest named Karol Wojtyla visited him in 1947. This, of course, was the man later to be known as JP II, who canonized St. Padre Pio.

St. Joan of Arc

For Your Holiness's Information

SAINTS FACTS

✤ The practice of naming saints began very early in the church's history, approximately A.D. 100. Many of the first named saints were martyrs who had died for the church.

✤ There are more than 10,000 saints and blessed, but the church lists no definitive head count of all of them.

✤ In his 26-year reign, JP II canonized hundreds of saints and oversaw nearly a thousand beatifications. In the 400 years before JP II, his predecessors presided over just 302 canonizations and 2,000 beatifications.

✤ Lengthy investigation that follows the nomination of a candidate for sainthood can cost upward of $100,000, which is paid by the nominating congregation or diocese.

✤ In the church canon, there are many saints with the same name, including 16 St. Anthonys. To keep them straight, these saints are given further identifications, such as their occupation (St. Anthony the Abbot) or personality (St. Anthony the Hermit).

✤ Patron saints are those chosen as special guardians over a given area of followers' lives. St. Francis of Assisi, for example, is the patron saint of ecologists, and St. Jude is the patron saint of lost causes. There is even a patron saint for TV, St. Claire of Assisi, who heard Christmas mass even though she was miles away from the church).

Essential Papal Knowledge

CONFIRMING MIRACLES

You will oversee the process whereby extraordinary events are officially determined to be miracles. Your judgments are critical because each nominee for sainthood is required to have performed at least two confirmed miracles. However, modern scientific advances have led to a clearer understanding of events that were once considered "miraculous," and the church's criteria for identifying miracles are stringent.

- The miracle most often still accepted is the divine cure of sickness, wherein a holy person heals a follower suffering from a serious illness, such as cancer or polio.
- After the healing has been performed, the entire process must be examined by a panel of 9 Italian doctors (chosen from a group of 100, known as the Consulta Medica), including experts in the field of the given disease. All must agree that the follower's cure was not simply medical or biological in nature.
- In 1969, the Vatican dropped 40 saints from the official catalog, after reappraising their credentials. In some cases, their miracles were discounted; in others doubts were raised about whether the person had actually existed.

For Your Holiness's Information
MIRACULOUS STORIES

On December 9, 1531, the Virgin Mary appeared to a humble man named Juan Diego, telling him to inform the local bishop to build a church right where she stood. Before building anything, though, the bishop demanded a sign that the vision was real. The Virgin Mother appeared again before Juan Diego and told him to gather roses, even though it was out of season for the flowers. Juan Diego did as he was told and when he returned to the bishop with the flowers, he let them spill from his cloak, revealing an image of the Holy Mother on the fabric. The bishop accepted the proof and the Chapel of the Indians was constructed in Mexico City. St. Juan Diego was canonized by JP II in 2002.

John Nepomucene Neumann, Philadelphia's bishop in the mid-nineteenth century, was granted sainthood in 1977 after several medicinal miracles were attributed to him, long after his death. In one case, a young child stricken with severe bone cancer was healed after St. Neumann's name was evoked—83 years after the bishop's death.

In Fatima, Portugal, in the early twentieth century, the Virgin Mary appeared to three small children, telling them to pray to the rosary and to make personal sacrifices. She also promised them a miracle on October 13, 1917. A huge crowd gathered to await her miracle on the appointed date, and they were not disappointed. Reportedly, the sun suddenly turned into a silver-like disk and started to dance in the sky.

Chapel of the Indians

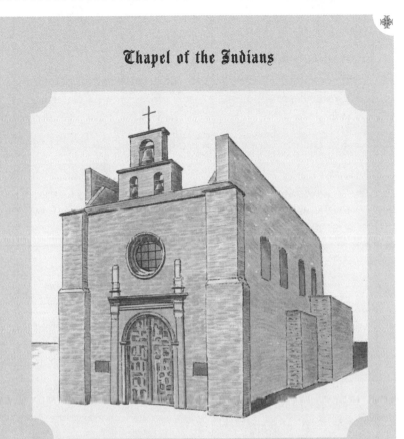

In 1992, a Peruvian submarine was sinking off the coast of South America when one of the crew prayed to Marija of Jesus Crucified, a Croatian nun, known widely for her good work in Latin America. After praying, the crewmember was able to close the bulkhead, ultimately saving more than 20 men from drowning.

CARDINAL STATS AND FACTS

+ Cardinals are appointed for life, unless they are elected pope.

+ The country with the largest tally of cardinals is Italy, with 20.

+ Western Europe accounts for nearly a third (46) of the total number of cardinals in the world, even though just 26.1% of Catholics live in Europe.

+ The average age of the cardinals is 71.7 years old.

+ The youngest cardinal ever appointed is believed to be Luis Antonio de Borbón, the 8-year-old son of King Felipe V of Spain, who, in 1735, insisted that his son be given the honor, which was bestowed by Clement XII. Louis held his cardinalship until he was 27, when he resigned so that he could marry.

+ The pontiff who created the most cardinals in his papacy was JP II, who appointed 231.

+ When an antipope creates cardinals, their official title is pseudocardinals.

+ Cardinals may sometimes be created in *pectore*, whereby the appointment is made but their names are not disclosed because of political reasons. Until they can be named publicly, they hold no official title or duties.

Essential Papal Knowledge

APPOINTING CARDINALS

Only you may decide who becomes a cardinal. Your decisions in this regard are far reaching and in many ways will determine the future character and direction of the church. Technically, you can appoint anyone you wish to be a cardinal, although tradition suggests certain limits: no modern pope could simply appoint a nonclergy relative, for example, without severe repercussions from the press and the church faithful. Whom you choose is critical.

✳ **Promote your vision.** Cardinals can have long careers. The individuals you choose can affect church policy for decades. They may in time occupy the most important curial positions and direct the most sensitive church bodies, such as the Congregation for the Doctrine of the Faith, which helps to establish official church doctrine. It's important that you choose not only competent managers but also representatives of your vision for the church's future.

✳ **Point the way for a successor.** Once they reach the age of 80, cardinals are not permitted to vote in the conclave. Because even recently appointed cardinals tend to be advanced in years, you may need to create a stream of new members just to keep the conclave's numbers steady.

The cardinals you appoint will play a part in deciding who becomes pontiff after you pass away. By extension, the next pope could be a cardinal you appoint. You could literally give a step-up to your eventual successor.

- **Reward merit.** Becoming a cardinal is an honor few clergymen ever receive. You may decide that certain church officials, even those beyond the age of 80, deserve the distinction as a reward for outstanding contribution to the faith.

- **Encourage your followers in newer, growing dioceses.** After you, cardinals are the public face of the church's senior ranks to followers around the world. The origins of whom you appoint sends a message, whether intended or not, about which regions of the world are important in church affairs. Choosing new cardinals from among clergy in regions outside Europe will underscore the church's universal mission.

Essential Papal Knowledge

WRITING ENCYCLICALS

Encyclicals are official letters you send to all your bishops around the world. They are intended to be made public. They expound on your particular philosophies and, therefore, are seen as guides to the official policies of the church on any number of religious topics and issues.

For Your Holiness's Information

CARDINALS BY GEOGRAPHY

Western Europe has the largest block of the 117 cardinals eligible to vote for a new pope.

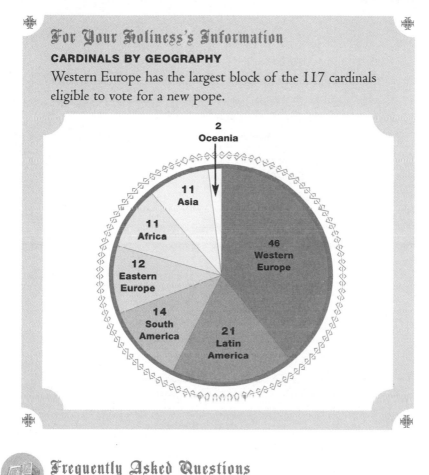

Frequently Asked Questions

WHO ACTUALLY DOES THE WRITING?

How encyclicals are written depends on how much of the writing you wish to do yourself. Pius XII, the first pontiff to use a typewriter, did much of his own writing. Other popes have told the Office of General Affairs what to research and have left them to actually flesh out their ideas. It's your call.

Frequently Asked Questions

WHO IS MY AUDIENCE?

Your encyclicals are intended to explain and set church doctrine, so all members of the church are your audience—they are meant to faithfully follow the doctrine the writings present. Every encyclical you write is laboriously translated into many different languages by an office in the Secretariat and distributed all over the world.

For Your Holiness's Information

THE SECRET ARCHIVES

Over the centuries, every pope has added to this hidden and ultra-secret library, which contains the facts, ideas, and opinions of the church.

- ✤ The Secret Archives are located in a fireproof, environmentally controlled area under the Pigna courtyard, outside the Vatican Museums.

- ✤ They reportedly contain 16 miles worth of shelves and hold the papers, books, and letters of many of the popes who have lived in the Vatican.

- ✤ Included are some of the most extraordinary private and personal papal documents, such as the appeal of King Henry VIII of England to Pope Clement VII for a divorce from Queen Catherine of Aragon and correspondence from such luminaries as Napoleon, Michelangelo, and Genghis Khan.

Frequently Asked Questions

WHAT SHOULD I WRITE ABOUT?

You may write on any subject you wish, even if that subject has been explored by a recent predecessor. In fact, you are encouraged to write your encyclicals on subjects that are of particular interest to you or that you feel need more official clarification.

Frequently Asked Questions

WHAT ARE APOSTOLIC LETTERS?

Apostolic letters are also public writings of yours, but rather than the much more far-reaching encyclical, they stay focused on a smaller, more particularized subject and are sent to a more specific audience.

EXCOMMUNICATIONS

You are responsible for enforcing church doctrine. Occasionally, you may be called upon to excommunicate a member of the church, although this is an increasingly rare punishment. Nevertheless, it remains the most severe penalty you can impose: total and absolute exclusion. The follower is still considered a Christian but is completely exiled and considered nonexistent until such time as the member sufficiently mends his or her ways and makes the appropriate absolution. Any member of the clergy may excommunicate someone in his parish, but you are given special excommunicating powers for specific crimes.

For Your Holiness's Information
SAMPLE EXCOMMUNICABLE CRIMES

✤ Attacking or wounding a member of the clergy or ordering the same.

✤ Committing heresy by rejecting the church's dogma.

✤ Reading the works of a heretic.

✤ Writing a false apostolic letter or brief as if from the hand of the pope (for nonpopes).

✤ Dueling or accepting the challenge of a duel.

✤ Becoming a Freemason.

 ## Frequently Asked Questions
DO I EVER PERFORM EXORCISMS?

It is possible that you may be brought in for particularly difficult cases. Pius XII had to intervene when Monsignor Balducci, one of only two clergy members on staff authorized by the pope to lead exorcisms, was able to rid one poor victim of just 9 of 10 demons inhabiting her body. When Pius XII appeared, the last demon finally disembarked, leaving her perfectly healthy.

Frequently Asked Questions

DOES THE CHURCH CHARGE A FEE FOR THIS SERVICE?

There is no fee. The service is performed free of charge for the victims, even when—in extreme cases—the exorcism rites have to continue for months at a time before the demon is eradicated.

EXORCISMS

Occasionally, one of your fellow Catholics may become possessed by a demon. Part of your job is to certify the training of priests and bishops who alleviate the suffering of the possessed church member by performing an exorcism.

✤ Exorcism is a rite that evokes a command from God for the demon to leave the body of its victim.

✤ The rite was indoctrinated by Paul V in 1614 and, except for the occasional light revision, has remained largely unchanged.

✤ An exorcism begins with a series of prayers and readings of the Psalms. This is followed by the reading of Gospel passages specifically concerned with possession as the exorcising priest makes the sign of the cross and places his right hand on the victim. A variety of other prayers are then used, including the Hail Mary.

✤ All prayers are made in Latin, since that is the demon's native tongue.

CHAPTER VI

Travel, Safety, and Security

✣

Before JP II, many popes spent a great deal of time ensconced in the Vatican, maintaining the order of the church from their office. Now, however, you will be expected to follow JP II's ambitious example (129 different nations visited) and travel all over the world as the church's main ambassador, almost constantly in the public eye. Of course, the pope must travel visibly but also securely. Because of these security concerns, a mountain of logistical problems must be solved before you may freely travel from one country to another. This is where your travel and security staff become absolutely essential members of your team.

THE POPEMOBILE

The most famous and beloved vehicle of its kind, the Popemobile has allowed many hundreds of thousands of the faithful catch a glimpse of their pontiff. The first such armored vehicle was manufactured by Land Rover after the assassination attempt on JP II in 1982. Mercedes Benz quickly followed with a version that surrounded the pontiff in bulletproof glass so that he could bless the giant crowds that attended his visits. Now there are no fewer than 20 Popemobiles situated all over the world. The Vatican itself houses 6 of the vehicles in its garage.

Frequently Asked Questions

WHAT DO THEY GET TO THE GALLON?

Fuel efficiency is not much of a factor when it comes to your Popemobile—your security is of chief concern. Fuel efficiency also depends somewhat on which model you happen to be driving in. But with the listed weight of most Popemobiles at an average of four tons (8,000 pounds), you can estimate that they would get roughly the same mileage as a comparably weighted Hummer H2, or approximately 9.6 miles per gallon.

Popemobile

 Frequently Asked Questions

WHAT IS MY LICENSE PLATE NUMBER?

With each of your vehicles, it is SCV I, which stands for Stato della Citta del Vaticano (State of Vatican City). Your license plate has red lettering on a white background; all other official SCV license plates use black lettering.

PAPAL AUTOMOBILES: STATS AND FACTS

❖ Besides Land Rover and Mercedes, the cars have been manufactured by Fiat, Renault, Peugeot, GM, Toyota, and Volkswagen.

❖ The astronomical cost of the cars is never disclosed as they are donated by the manufacturers.

❖ Before the armored Popemobiles, popes were often transported in ornate carriages, several of which are displayed in the Vatican Carriage Museum. Shortly after the automobile was introduced, the Vatican acquired some particularly resplendent models. Pope Pius XI was fond of Isotta Fraschini limousines, while his successor, Pius XII, had several Cadillacs designed solely for his use, including one that had an adjustable throne. He was also given a Bianchi, a Fiat 525, and a Graham-Paige. With cars like these, it's no wonder Pius XII could be heard to yell "Velocita, velocita" (faster, faster) to his chauffeur.

❖ In addition to bulletproof glass, the engines of the Popemobiles are covered by steel plates and the transmissions are specially designed to enable the driver to accelerate very quickly in forward or reverse if need be.

❖ Ferrari made a Formula I car for JP II on the occasion of his twenty-sixth year as pontiff, a scaled-down version of their regular F2004. Despite other suggestions, they kept the car the same shade of red as a regular Ferrari.

TRAVELING ABROAD

Planning the papal visit abroad is an incredibly complex and difficult task, involving the full efforts of a large support staff, headed by your personal secretary. Any papal visit abroad can take up to two years of careful planning, working with the host country, so that all logistical and security concerns are properly dealt with to the satisfaction of all concerned.

Frequently Asked Questions
DO I HAVE A PLANE?

While there is no specific papal plane—when flying, you use a chartered jet—there is an official heliport in the VC. It stands on a former tennis court and was dubbed "the helicoptorum" by John XXIII. The Papalcopter then whisks you away to either one of the major Roman airports (the Ciampino for trips within Italy, the Fiumcino for visits abroad) or your summer retreat at Castel Gandolfo.

Frequently Asked Questions
HOW DOES THE CHURCH PAY FOR THIS?

The church actually doesn't pay for much of the travel costs: the host country is responsible for your travel expenses, room and board, and, most important, your large security needs. In order for this arrangement to work in any country that has a separation of church and state, the papacy must be recognized as both a religious and political organization. The host country is often responsible not just for the basic travel expenses, but also for all the street closures, traffic rerouting, and police overtime.

Frequently Asked Questions

DO I HAVE A TRAVEL AGENT? WHO PLANS THE ITINERARY?

No one travel agent could handle all the logistics that go into a papal visit. A special papal delegation is sent to the prospective host country long before your travel date is set. Together, they plan out your travel route, including which specific cities you will be visiting. Once this process is completed, which can take anywhere from several months to several years, your itinerary is worked out very meticulously by your head secretary and his staff.

Frequently Asked Questions

DO I HAVE A PASSPORT?

Yes, you have one of the few passports issued from the VC: the white Holy See Number I.

Frequently Asked Questions

DO I HAVE TO STAND IN LINE AT CUSTOMS?

As the highest-ranking leader for the VC, an independent state, you are given diplomatic immunity in your travels,

KISSING THE GROUND

When you first disembark onto the ground of a new country, the act of kissing the ground is meant as a sign of deep reverence and humility toward the people of the land. As you know, in church doctrine, a kiss is an extremely significant sign of respect, such as when a bishop bows and kisses your fisherman's ring. Here you are telling the inhabitants of the country that you come as but a humble servant.

Pope Kissing
the Ground

allowing you to forgo the usual customs and security checkpoints that are common for a regular international traveler.

Essential Papal Knowledge

PAPAL ETIQUETTE

With all eyes on you, you have to maintain your regal and dignified countenance at all times. This includes your choice of activities (nothing that would flout the sanctioned activities of the church) and wardrobe. While traveling as a dignitary of the church, you must always wear your official vestments, or a variation thereof, although exceptions are made in extreme circumstances. There are, for example, white papal parkas available for your use in cold weather. White sneakers or boots may also be substituted for your red shoes under particularly frigid weather conditions.

Frequently Asked Questions

CAN I WEAR SUNGLASSES?

Although most often you do not want to wear anything to obscure your eyes from members of the church for fear of seeming aloof, there might be occasions when donning sunglasses is necessary. JP II famously appropriated a pair of fashionable sunglasses from U2 lead singer Bono during a visit the rock frontman made to Castel Gandolfo. The pontiff wanted to wear them during his daily walks in the papal gardens under the bright Italian sun.

Essential Papal Knowledge

SECURITY

As a worldwide religious icon, you have to be prepared for people who want to bring you to harm as a way of making a political statement. In today's delicate political and religious environment, the stakes are higher than ever. In order to protect you, there is an elite security force at your beck and call.

SWISS GUARDS

It is the job of the Swiss Guards to protect you against all enemies, at the risk of their own lives. Normally, they patrol the three main entrances of the Vatican, as well as the Apostolic Palace, in the hallway right outside your apartment, 24 hours a day. They also guard you at Castel Gandolfo and help protect you on your international trips.

- ❖ You appoint the commander of the Guards, whose rank is always colonel. He is part of your immediate hierarchy, and is given the title "Chamberlain of His Holiness."

- ❖ At 100 members, the Guards remain the world's smallest standing army.

- ❖ New recruits initially sign on to serve a two-year tour of duty. This short service cycle places enormous pressure on the Guards to find and train new candidates, since not all members choose to reenlist. (*continued on page 107*)

HISTORY OF THE SWISS GUARDS

✣ The Swiss Guards were founded in 1506 by Pope Julius II, who was greatly impressed with the Swiss military. He brought in 150 elite Swiss soldiers to become his personal military corps and actually led them into battle more than once against the French occupation until Italy was restored.

✣ The guards were very nearly wiped out of existence by an enormous group of German and Spanish mercenaries sent out by the Holy Roman Emperor Charles V in 1527. The mercenaries stormed the steps of St. Peter's, killing 147 of the Guards, including the commanding officer and his wife. The remaining Guards still managed to hold off the hordes long enough for Pope Clement VII and many of his cardinals to escape.

✣ The distinctive, brightly colored uniforms were designed by a Vatican seamstress, on commission for Benedict XV in 1914. It is said that the seamstress was inspired by a Raphael painting.

✣ The date of the Guards' heroic effort against Charles V, May 6, is the day all new recruits take their oath to serve and protect the pope. Many retired Guards visit the Vatican as part of the formal proceedings.

Swiss Guard

For Your Holiness's Information

VATICAN SECRET SERVICE

The VSS is the intelligence-gathering arm of the Vatican, employing a small number of agents as full-time spies. In recent times, however, the efforts of the VSS have mainly been to keep other spies out of the Vatican.

✤ A growing part of the VSS's responsibilities is keeping the Vatican clear of bugs, especially during a conclave.

✤ The use of cell phones and other electronic devices is outlawed during a conclave for fear that the devices can be hacked and then used to eavesdrop on the proceedings.

✤ The VSS has to perform a regular and extremely thorough search for bugs, checking not just the furniture, walls, and drapes, but also the electrical wiring, light fixtures, and plumbing.

✤ During the 2005 conclave, all the cardinals were searched for electronic devices before they were allowed to enter the sacred chamber and begin the process of selecting a new pope.

(*continued from page 103*)

✣ New Guards must be between 18 and 25 years old and be at least six feet tall.

✣ Once they join the unit, recruits are trained in sword and halberd fighting, exactly as their forebears were. They are also required to maintain excellent physical fitness and are trained in modern weaponry and modern counter-terrorism techniques.

✣ They are armed with seven-foot halberds and, during formal occasions, they wear breastplates and helmets festooned with large ostrich feathers.

✣ Jewelry, long hair, and the sporting of any kind of beard or mustache are forbidden.

✣ Marriage is not permitted during their first few years of service, and Guards are not allowed to bring any friends into their Vatican living quarters.

✣ While patrolling the Vatican, the Swiss Guards are not permitted to use guns, which were banned by Paul VI in 1970. Instead, they use their halberds to defend the Holy See.

✣ Every year, new recruits take their oath to serve and protect the pope on May 6—the day of the Guards' heroic effort against Charles V's mercenary armies in 1527.

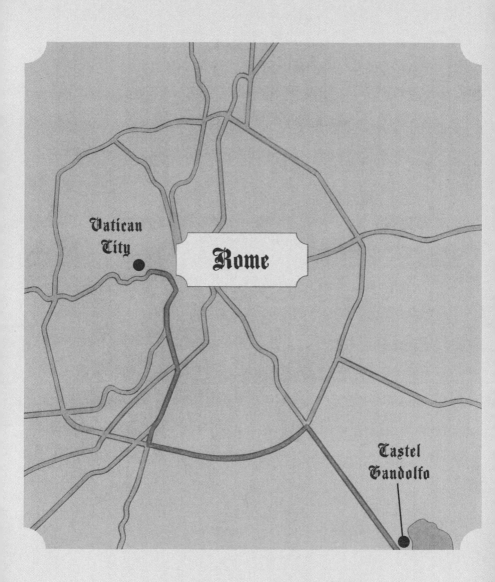

Vatican
City

Rome

Castel
Gandolfo

CHAPTER VII

Rest and Recreation

Even the pope is entitled to some downtime. With such a demanding job and relentless hours, you'll need a chance to unwind and relax from the stresses of the office. Your main getaway is the papal retreat at Castel Gandolfo, just 13 miles south of Rome in the Alban Hills, where you can take your summers to avoid the Roman heat. But there are other options as well, from the gym and spa in the VC, to the VC bowling alley and billiards rooms, to the fabulous art stored in the Vatican Museums. And if you ever want to bring in a friend from outside the church, you have plenty of guest accommodations for him or her.

Essential Papal Knowledge
RELAXATION

Through the ages, pontiffs have used different methods to unwind. JP II, an avid outdoorsman, enjoyed hiking in the mountains and swimming, while Pius XI was more of a full-blown mountaineer, ascending both the Matterhorn and Mont Blanc. He also kept 16 cars in the Vatican garage for his personal use, 3 of which were convertibles. Pius IX, meanwhile, loved billiards, playing against other cardinals and Swiss Guards as much as he could. Julius II loved water and spent most of his free time on boats. As long as it's not too dangerous and in keeping with the papal image, you are free to follow your recreational desires.

✤ A small gym is housed in the Apostolic Palace, where you can go to do a few minutes on a Stairmaster or lift weights.

✤ John XXIII installed a bowling alley that is regularly used by members of the clergy. When he wasn't on the lanes, John XXIII also greatly enjoyed going to the terrace apartment of the tallest building in the Vatican— the Tower of the Winds—and watch the goings-on in the Roman streets through a pair of binoculars.

✤ In addition to the regular papal gardens, which are open to the public, you have a private garden on the roof of the Apostolic Palace, directly above your papal apartment. The trellised garden includes fountains and a false roof so no one can observe you when you are enjoying its beauty.

𝔉requently 𝔄sked ℭuestions
CAN I MAINTAIN A ROOTING INTEREST IN A SPORT?

Sport has long been a part of the Vatican. In fact, JP II insisted that the ceremony installing him as pontiff be held early enough so that he could watch an important soccer match on TV. Pius XII was such a soccer fan that his cardinals joked that the only way they could get to see him was if they dressed as players. The Vatican fields a team for international matches but there is also a soccer league in the VC, whose teams include the ACV (Vatican Catholic Association), DIRESCO (Economic Services Office), and Meridiana (Secret Archives).

𝔉requently 𝔄sked ℭuestions
CAN MY FRIENDS COME TO VISIT?

Your friends are welcome to visit you at the Vatican. While visiting, they can stay at your well-appointed alternative papal apartment in the Vatican at St. John's Tower. This is also where you stay when your regular apartment is being remodeled.

Frequently Asked Questions

AM I ALLOWED TO KEEP A PET?

Even though there is a rule on the books that caged birds and animals are not allowed in the VC, the short answer is that, yes, pets are permitted. And historically pontiffs have kept quite a few pets. Birds have been very popular: Pius XII had a pet canary named Gretchen who hopped onto his shoulder as soon as she was released from her cage, and several popes have kept parrots, including Martin V and Pius II. Meanwhile, Julius III had pet monkeys and Leo X famously owned a white elephant named Hanno, to the consternation of Martin Luther, who disapproved of the pontiff displaying Hanno so proudly on the streets of Rome. Fearing that kind of negative attention, Leo XII made do with just a small dog.

Frequently Asked Questions

CAN I HAVE A DRINK?

JP II took an occasional glass of Tuscan red wine. Pius XII, meanwhile, drank at least one glass of red wine every day, even going so far as to bring a personal flask with him when he traveled.

Frequently Asked Questions

WHAT'S IN THE PAPAL MOVIE COLLECTION?

What you choose to watch is, of course, up to you. But back in 1995, on the 100th anniversary of cinema, the Vatican released its list of the films it considered "great." The films were divided into three categories: religion, values, and art.

✤ **The religion category** included such films as *Ben-Hur*, *The Mission*, *Babette's Feast*, and *The Passion of Joan of Arc*, a silent film from 1928.

✤ **The values category** included *The Bicycle Thief*, *Chariots of Fire*, *Gandhi*, *It's a Wonderful Life*, *On the Waterfront*, and *Schindler's List*.

✤ **The art category** had a range of films, including *Citizen Kane*, *8½*, *Nosferatu*, *Fantasia*, *2001: A Space Odyssey*, and *The Wizard of Oz*.

ART IN THE VC

After nearly two millennia of some of the finest artists in the world working for the church, you can sample some pretty impressive work, none more so than Michelangelo's sublime work in the Sistine Chapel. There is an almost limitless variety of art objects accessible to you as pope, from Greek sculptures and Renaissance art, including paintings by Giotto, Caravaggio, and Poussin, among many others.

SISTINE CHAPEL

Contrary to popular belief, there is far more to see here than just Michelangelo's world-famous ceiling.

---

* The stories of Moses (south walls) and Christ (north walls) and the portraits of the pontiffs (south, north, and entrance walls) were all painted by a team consisting of Pietro Perugino, Sandro Botticelli, Domenico Ghirlandaio, and Cosimo Rosselli and their respective assistants. The work was commissioned by Sixtus IV, completed in the fifteenth century, and consecrated in August of 1483.

* The ceiling consists of nine central stories, illustrating different narratives from Genesis, from the Creation to the Fall and then the Flood and mankind's subsequent rebirth. It took Michelangelo four years to complete the ceiling, after being commissioned by Julius II in May of 1508.

* The finished chapel was inaugurated on the Feast of All Saints (November 1) in 1512.

* The success of the ceiling prompted another pontiff, Clement VII, to solicit Michelangelo to paint the Last Judgment on the altar wall in 1533. The painting was started in 1536 and took the artist five years to complete.

* To avenge himself against a clergyman who had reprimanded him for drawing nude bodies in the Last Judgment, Michelangelo painted a likeness of him in the corner of the work, giving him the ears of a donkey.

The
Sistine Chapel

Frequently Asked Questions

WHAT DOES THE VATICAN DO WITH ALL ITS BAD ART?

The Vatican may be known for its resplendent collection of
brilliant masterworks, but it also has a number of less than
memorable artifacts. These are kept in a warehouse-like
converted palace called the Floreria, which also acts as the
office in charge of decoration. In this huge space, you will
find old thrones, flaking busts of mostly unrecognizable
cardinals, poorly made statues of the Virgin Mary, used and
worn-out furniture from past pontiffs, and a massive collection of truly bad paintings, many given to the Vatican as gifts.

Frequently Asked Questions

CAN I VISIT THE ART?

You can visit the art as much as you wish. On the second floor of the Apostolic Palace exists one of the greatest collections of art in the world: the Raphael Rooms, four rooms filled with Raphael frescoes and paintings. Next to the Sistine Chapel, they are considered the most priceless pieces in the Vatican collection.

RECREATIONAL ATTIRE

There are limits to protocol. When you want to get in a workout, you can't do it in flowing robes. Although your color scheme should remain minimal (white or, on occasion, black), you may wear the gym apparel appropriate to the sport.

Frequently Asked Questions

DOES THE POPE EVER DRESS AS A CIVILIAN?

As far as civilian clothing is concerned, the current law isn't quite as stringent as it used to be. Back in 1884, it was decreed that clergy members "... at home or when engaged in the sanctuary" should "... always wear the cassock ..." Although you are required to wear your official papal vestments and outfits on all church business (unless you are traveling incognito for security purposes), when on vacation or in repose, you have a bit more flexibility. For example, JP II, who was an avid skier, would wear proper ski attire—even snow pants—on the slopes. He would, however, choose the priest's all-black color scheme as opposed to his normal papal white, so he would be safely visible to other skiers.

PAPAL RETREAT

The papal vacation home since 1626, the Castel Gandolfo hillside residence and farm is set in the Alban Hills 15 miles from the VC and is a great getaway, as the cooling winds coming off Albano Lake provide a much more hospitable environment than Rome in the summertime. Typically, you will spend most of August and September in the Castel's cooler climes. This is not strictly a vacation, however. You will be expected to more or less maintain your regular papal schedule while you are there, meeting with dignitaries and tending to the business of the church.

Frequently Asked Questions

DO I GET A REGULAR VACATION?

It is not uncommon for the pontiff to sneak away for a weekend several times a season. JP II loved to go hiking and skiing in the Italian Alps whenever he could. You can take a longer break (up to two weeks at a time) at least once a year. You'll hardly be out on your own, traveling with a large staff, but at least you'll get to enjoy a different part of the world.

CASTEL GANDOLFO FACTS

* The residence is enormous and sits within a 136-acre estate that is 29 acres larger than the VC itself. It covers almost the entire length of the small town it resides in.

* A permanent staff of 100 tends the residence. In addition to the permanent staff, you travel with your personal staff of nuns, your secretarial staff, your chamberlain, and 17 Swiss Guards who keep watch over the enormous gardens.

* A special building surrounded by perfectly manicured shrubbery serves as your meeting place for visiting VIPs and dignitaries.

* The spectacular gardens are accessible to you via an elevated walkway, allowing you to avoid having to cross the street.

* An avid swimmer, JP II had a special papal pool built on one of the terraces, allowing you the chance for a refreshing dip any time of day. You just need to be wary of the relentless paparazzi, who famously managed to get a shot of JP II in his swimming suit—a fair scandal at the time.

* The papal farm is just nearby, providing you with fresh fruits, vegetables, and dairy products year-round.

* The papal observatory is also housed within the confines of the residence, allowing you and your guests access to

Castel Gandolfo

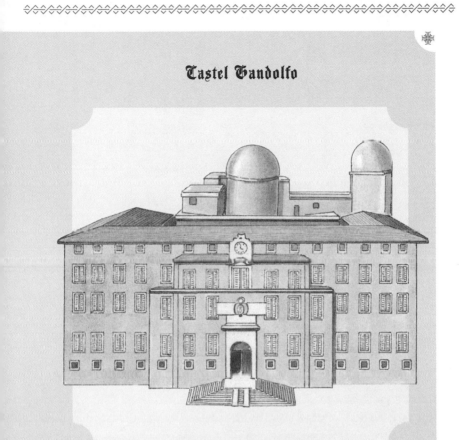

the heavens without the disruptive lights of Rome to spoil the view.

✴ During WWII, the villa was used to hide Jewish families escaping from the Germans. Pius XII reportedly housed thousands of escapees, shielding them from the Nazis.

Appendices

I. TERMS OF EMPLOYMENT
Compensation

The pontiff receives no salary. You do have use of all the amenities and resources of the VC and Castel Gandolfo, and your room and board is covered. You also receive 24-hour security and the use of the Popemobiles, and your international visits and vacations are all paid for by the church and the host countries.

Medical Benefits

You are fully covered against infirmity, in whatever country you happen to take ill or have an accident. Your medical coverage extends to any length of hospital stay anywhere in the world.

Retirement

The pontiff is able to resign—or, officially, abdicate—although there have only been approximately 10 resignations during the 2,000-year history of the position. The most recent resignation was by Gregory XII, at the end of the fifteenth century, but the code of canon law, most recently overseen by JP II in 1996, allows a pope to resign, as long as it is his own decision and he is of sound mind.

The church's book of canon law (sec. 332.2) states, "If it should happen that the Roman Pontiff resigns his office, it is required for validity that he make the resignation freely and that it be duly manifested, but not that it be accepted by anyone."

If you were to resign, you would remain as either a bishop or a cardinal, although you would lose your power of infallibility, which belongs to the office, not the individual. You would retain your medical coverage and be given your room and board, although it would not be in the papal apartment.

Additional Sources

The following sources can be accessed for further information:

BOOKS

Accattoli, Luigi, and Galazka, Grzegorz. *Life in the Vatican with John Paul II.* New York: Universe Publishing, 1998.

Allen, John L., Jr. *All the Pope's Men.* New York: Doubleday, 2004.

Hardon, John A. *Pocket Catholic Dictionary.* New York: Image Books, 1985.

Hofmann, Paul. *O Vatican!* New York: Congdon & Weed, 1984.

Kerr, William Shaw. *A Handbook on the Papacy.* London: Marshall Morgan & Scott, 1950.

Lo Bello, Nino. *The Incredible Book of Vatican Facts and Papal Curiosities.* Union Town: Liguori Publications, 1998.

Reese, Thomas J. *Inside the Vatican.* Cambridge, Mass.: Harvard University Press, 1996.

Williams, Paul L. *The Vatican Exposed.* Amherst, Mass.: Prometheus Books, 2003.

PERIODICALS

The New York Times
Newsweek
The Philadelphia Inquirer
The Wall Street Journal

WEB SITES

www.totalcatholic.com
www.catholic-pages.com
www.infoplease.com
www.rc.net
www.vatican.va

Index

Page numbers in italics
indicate illustrations